Bees /
J595.79 Pri   147269

Prischmann, Deirdre A.
Wilton Public Library

DATE DUE

World of Insects

Bees

by Deirdre A. Prischmann

Consultant:
Gary A. Dunn, MS, Director of Education
Young Entomologists' Society, Inc.
Minibeast Zooseum and Education Center
Lansing, Michigan

Capstone press
Mankato, Minnesota

Bridgestone Books are published by Capstone Press,
151 Good Counsel Drive, P.O. Box 669, Mankato, Minnesota 56002.
www.capstonepress.com

Library of Congress Cataloging-in-Publication Data
Prischmann, Deirdre A.
    Bees / by Deirdre A. Prischmann.
      p. cm.—(Bridgestone Books. World of insects)
    Summary: "A brief introduction to bees, discussing their characteristics, habitat, life cycle, and predators. Includes a range map, life cycle illustration, and amazing facts"—Provided by publisher.
    Includes bibliographical references and index.
    ISBN 0-7368-4334-5 (hardcover)
    1. Bees—Juvenile literature. I. Title. II. Series: World of insects.
QL565.2.P75 2006
595.79'9—dc22   2004028430

Editorial Credits

Shari Joffe, editor; Jennifer Bergstrom, set designer; Biner Design, book designer;
    Patricia Rasch, illustrator; Jo Miller, photo researcher; Scott Thoms, photo editor

Photo Credits

Bill Johnson, 12
Bruce Coleman Inc./J.C. Carton, 6; Kim Taylor, 20; Larry West, 1
Dwight R. Kuhn, 18
Pete Carmichael, 4
Peter Arnold, Inc./Hans Pfletschinger, 16
Root Resources/Jim Nachel, 10
Steven J. Meunier, cover

1 2 3 4 5 6 10 09 08 07 06 05

Table of Contents

Bees 5

What Bees Look Like 7

Bees in the World 9

Bee Habitats 11

What Bees Eat 13

Eggs and Larvae 15

Pupae and Adults 17

Dangers to Bees 19

Amazing Facts about Bees 21

Glossary 22

Read More 23

Internet Sites 23

Index 24

4

Bees

Bees are known for their stings, but they should be known for helping give us many foods. As bees feed from flowers, they get **pollen** on their bodies. They spread the pollen from flower to flower. This action helps plants make more plants. Without bees, we wouldn't have as many fruits and vegetables.

Bees are insects. They are related to hornets, wasps, and ants. All insects have six legs, three body parts, and an **exoskeleton**. The exoskeleton protects and supports an insect's body.

◄ Bees get covered in sticky pollen, then carry it from plant to plant.

What Bees Look Like

Bees come in many colors and sizes. They can be black, yellow, or even green. Some are not much larger than a pinhead. Others are longer than a pin.

A bee's body has three parts. The head is one part. It has eyes, **antennae**, and mouthparts. A bee's legs and four wings join to the middle part, or **thorax**. The end part is the **abdomen**. Female bees have stingers at the ends of their abdomens.

◄ All bees have feather-like hairs on their bodies.

Bee Range Map

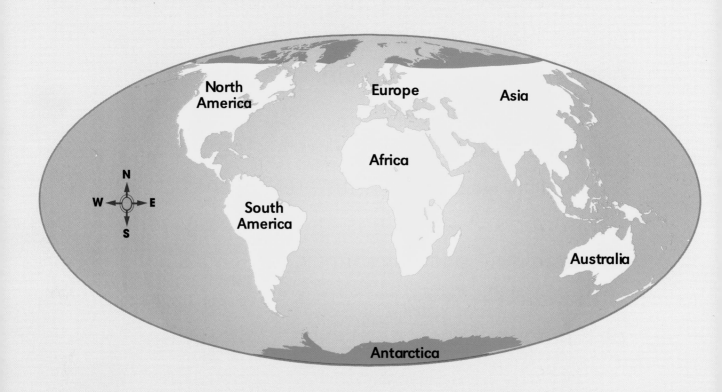

North America

Europe

Asia

Africa

South America

Australia

Antarctica

N
W E
S

☐ Where Bees Live

Bees in the World

More than 20,000 kinds of bees live in the world. These include honey bees, bumble bees, sweat bees, and leafcutter bees.

Bees live wherever flowering plants grow. Large numbers of flowering plants grow in tropical rain forests. Many bees live in these warm, wet areas.

Some bees live in cold places, including high mountain peaks. The North and South poles are the only places that are too cold for bees.

Bee Habitats

Most kinds of bees are **solitary**. Female solitary bees raise their young by themselves. They make simple nests in wood, plant stems, or the ground. Some leafcutter bees use empty snail shells for nests.

Other bees, including honey bees, live together in groups called colonies. Colonies live in large nests or hives. The bees in a colony work together to gather food and raise young bees. Bumble bees often live in underground colonies.

◄ Honey bees usually build their nests in trees. A nest may contain as many as 60,000 bees.

What Bees Eat

Bees get their food from flowers. They feed on sweet flower nectar and pollen. Bees use their tongue-like mouthparts to drink nectar. Most bees carry pollen in special "pollen baskets" on their legs. Other bees carry pollen on the underside of their abdomens.

Bees bring the food back to their nests. Young bees eat pollen and nectar in the nest. Honey bees store nectar as honey. These bees eat the honey in winter, when there are no flowers.

◀ Bumble bees and many other bees put pollen in special "baskets" on their hind legs.

The Life Cycle of a Bee

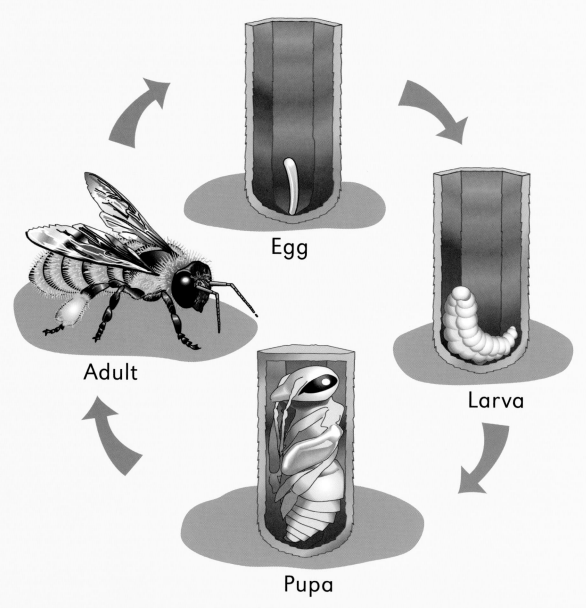

Egg

Larva

Pupa

Adult

Eggs and Larvae

Male and female bees mate to produce eggs. Female bees lay eggs in small cells inside their nests. Bee colonies have one female bee that lays all the eggs. She is called the queen bee.

Larvae hatch from eggs after a few days. Larvae look very different from adults. They are soft and don't have legs. As the larvae grow, they **molt**, or shed their exoskeleton, four or five times.

Pupae and Adults

A larva soon grows to fill its cell. Then it changes into a **pupa**. At first, bee pupae look like larvae. Later, bee pupae look more like white adults. When a pupa becomes a true adult, it climbs out of its cell.

Honey bees change from eggs to adults in about 20 days. Carpenter bees take about 36 days. Mason bees can take 97 days.

As adults, bees live for different lengths of time. Some live only a few days. Queen honey bees often live for three years.

A honey bee pupa grows in its cell. Bees live in their cells during the egg, larval, and pupal stages.

Dangers to Bees

Bees face many dangers. Birds, spiders, skunks, and wasps eat adult bees. Bears try to steal honey from honey bee colonies. Sprays that people use to kill crop pests can hurt bees as they gather pollen and nectar.

A bee's main defense is its stinger. Bees won't sting unless they feel threatened. Some bees can sting only once, while others are able to sting several times. So watch out! Don't bug any bees.

◄ A female honey bee loses its stinger and dies after it stings.

Amazing Facts about Bees

- Worker honey bees create new queens by feeding certain larvae a special food called royal jelly.
- Honey bees communicate with each other. They do dances to tell other bees where to find food.
- A bee's buzz is the sound of its wings beating. The wings of a honey bee beat up to 11,400 times per minute.
- Not all bees sting. Male bees don't have stingers. Tropical stingless bees also don't have stingers.

◄ The queen (center) is the biggest bee in a honey bee colony. Worker bees take care of her at all times.

Glossary

abdomen (AB-duh-muhn)—the end section of an insect's body

antenna (an-TEN-uh)—a feeler on an insect's head

exoskeleton (eks-oh-SKEL-uh-tuhn)—the hard outer covering of an insect

larva (LAR-vuh)—an insect at the stage after an egg; more than one larva are larvae.

molt (MOHLT)—to shed an outer layer of skin, or exoskeleton, so a new exoskeleton can be seen

pollen (PAHL-un)—tiny grains made by many plants

pupa (PYOO-puh)—an insect at the stage of development between a larva and an adult; more than one pupa are pupae.

solitary (SOL-uh-ter-ee)—alone; solitary bees make their own nests and do not live in colonies.

thorax (THOR-aks)—the middle section of an insect's body; wings and legs are attached to the thorax.

Read More

Birch, Robin. *Bees Up Close.* Minibeasts Up Close. Chicago: Raintree, 2005.

Hodge, Deborah. *Bees.* Tonawanda, N.Y.: Kids Can Press, 2004.

Internet Sites

FactHound offers a safe, fun way to find Internet sites related to this book. All of the sites on FactHound have been researched by our staff.

Here's how:
1. Visit *www.facthound.com*
2. Type in this special code **0736843345** for age-appropriate sites. Or enter a search word related to this book for a more general search.
3. Click on the **Fetch It** button.

FactHound will fetch the best sites for you!

Index

abdomen, 7, 13
antennae, 7

body parts, 5, 7, 13

colonies, 11, 15, 19, 21

dangers, 19

eating, 13
eggs, 15, 17
exoskeleton, 5, 15
eyes, 7

flowers, 5, 9, 13
food, 5, 11, 13, 21

habitats, 9, 11
hives, 11
honey, 13, 19

larvae, 15, 17, 21
legs, 5, 7, 13, 15
life cycle, 15, 17

mating, 15
molting, 15
mouthparts, 7, 13

nectar, 13, 19
nests, 11, 13, 15

plants, 5, 9, 11
pollen, 5, 13, 19
pollen baskets, 13
pupae, 17

queen, 15, 17, 21

range, 9

size, 7
sting, 5, 7, 19, 21

thorax, 7

wings, 7, 21